Thank You for your
support and I pray
that this book will
be a blessing to you
and your family.

Thomas H S
II Tim 2:15

Special thanks to the Lord for the gift of salvation and for freely giving His knowledge and wisdom, meeting every need and answering my prayers according to His perfect will.

I want to thank my beloved wife and children for their support, encouragement, and patience through the process of writing this book. Thank you to those who have proofread this book.

Thank you to Professional Support Staff—especially to Gayle Washington and Diana Spurgin who has worked with me from start to finish to get this book published.

Table of Contents

Introduction 1

Building on Good Ground/Foundations 4

Purpose of Dedicating Your Children unto the Lord 11

Conducting Devotions with Your Children 13

Teaching Your Children How to Select Friends 20

Listening to Our Children 24

Tips on Disciplining 29

Pointing Our Children in the Direction of the Lord 38

Guidelines for Choosing Good Christian Music 40

Communication between Parents and Their Children 43

Having a Godly View of Our Children 46

Encouraging Our Children To Do What Is
Right Publicly and Privately 50

Weeding Out Jealousy between Siblings 53

Cultivating a Sincere Heart of Apology 57

Expressing Love to Our Children 60

Building Self-Confidence 62

Authority in the Home 64

Teaching Siblings How to Get Along 65

"And, ye fathers, **provoke not your children to wrath: but bring them up in the nurture and admonition of the Lord.**" (Ephesians 6:4)

Tips for Raising Our Children for the Lord!

Tips: Small but Useful Pieces of Practical Advice

Written by Thomas A. Symonette

"Correct thy son, and he shall give thee rest; yea, he shall give delight unto thy soul." (Proverbs 29:17)

"Train up a child in the way he should go: and when he is old, he will not depart from it." (Proverbs 22:6)

"We cannot be casual concerning our parenting; rather, we need to be deliberate."

Introduction

This book may help you in certain areas to establish a small foundation on which to build, but neither this book nor any other book can ever replace the Bible, which is the Word of God. The Bible is the only book that holds all of the answers. These answers are truly accessible when you know Jesus Christ as your personal Lord and Savior. If you seek after the wisdom that only God can give, He will give it to you.

The Bible says in Proverbs 2:1-9,

> My son, if thou wilt receive my words, and hide my commandments with thee; So that thou incline thine ear unto wisdom, and apply thine heart to understanding; Yea, if thou criest after knowledge, and liftest up thy voice for understanding; If thou seekest her as silver, and searchest for her as for hid treasures; Then shalt thou understand the fear of the Lord, and find the knowledge of God. For the Lord giveth wisdom: out of his mouth cometh knowledge and understanding. He layeth up sound wisdom for the righteous: he is a buckler to them that walk uprightly. He keepeth the paths of judgment, and preserveth the way of his saints. Then shalt thou understand righteousness, and judgment, and equity; yea, every good path.

As I have reared my beloved children, God has provided me with the knowledge and wisdom to deal effectively with every situation and every stage they have gone through. I have also applied that knowledge and wisdom toward children I worked with in child development centers, as well as other programs, and I have experienced success working with those children. Some had behavioral issues and various types of special needs. Many of the children came from diverse cultural backgrounds and nonconventional families.

It is my desire to help parents experience the success that God wants them to have in the area of raising their children for the Lord and building strong, healthy relationships with their children. I don't deal in this book with the topics of suicide, sexual preference, lust, masturbation, depression, and how to aid youth that struggle with sin, but because of the foundational principles in this book I have been able to assist and have open conversations with youth about these topics. With the right foundation, you can have deep talks with your children, and they can open up to you. And because of the things I share with you in this book, I am able to talk with my children and they are comfortable talking to me.

We need to understand that God is the master builder. Without Him, everything that we labor to do is in vain, but with Him we are able to build strong families, churches, communities, and relationships with others. The Bible says in Psalm 127:1, "Except the Lord build the house, they labour in vain that build it: except the Lord keep the city, the watchman waketh but in vain." The word *vain* in this context means "uselessness."

God is the architect—the master builder. God has provided all the materials necessary for us to build good Christian homes when we follow His plan and use the materials that He has provided. But if we choose not to follow or obey God, we cannot experience the success that God wants us to have within our homes. This applies not only to our homes, but to other areas of our lives as well. If we decide to do it our own way, we will labor in vain, like the watchman in Psalm 127:1. But if God is in it, God can enable us to have good success.

"I can do all things through Christ which strengtheneth me." (Philippians 4:13)

"For it is God which worketh in you both to will and to do of his good pleasure." (Philippians 2:13)

Think about this scripture from Joshua 1:8:

> This book of the law shall not depart out of thy mouth; but thou shalt meditate therein day and night, that thou mayest observe to do according to all that is written therein: for then thou shalt make thy way prosperous, and then thou shalt have good success.

When you read and study the Word of God and then apply it to your life, you can have good success according to the will of God. Take a moment to think about this statement: ***"God is a God of unconditional love, but He has conditional promises."*** God will respond to us as we obey Him. It is God's will for us to have good Christian homes; He doesn't want us to lose our children to the world.

Building on Good Ground/ Foundations

Life is filled with physical and non-physical foundations. Our relationships with others will grow stronger when they are built upon a foundation of truth. The opposite is also true: relationships can be ruined and destroyed when built on a foundation of deceit. Foundations are being developed all around us. Without the proper foundation, a structure cannot be properly constructed. If something is improperly built, that structure under the right circumstances will fall.

We need a proper foundation of faith that is built on the Rock—the Lord Jesus Christ. Through that healthy relationship with our Lord, all other areas will be affected in a positive manner, including our relationships with our families and with our peers. We can experience increased spiritual growth and wisdom, along with the ability to raise children that honor God and their parents through the testimony of their lives.

What type of foundation are you laying down and building upon in your life? What type of foundations are you laying down and building upon in the lives of your children? Christ cautions us, "For which of you, intending to build a tower, sitteth not down first, and counteth the cost, whether he have sufficient to finish it? . . . Or what king, going to make war against another king, sitteth not down first, and consulteth whether he be able with ten thousand to meet him that cometh against him with twenty thousand?" (Luke 14:28, 31). The Bible also says in Proverbs 29:18, "Where there is no vision the people perish: but he that keepeth the law, happy is he."

Do you have a vision of what type of men or women you want your children to grow into? Do you have a plan for how you can help them to become those individuals? As you read the Bible and seek the Lord in this matter of raising your children, God will show His vision and how to bring it to fruition.

*We cannot be casual concerning our parenting; rather, we need to be deliberate. We have to recognize that we are not on our own because there is a God that knows what has to be done. There is a God who has given us an instruction manual (the Bible) and who will give insight and wisdom if you ask Him (James 1:5). I want to encourage you to sit down and take some time to seriously consider what you want to impart to your children and how you are going to implement that plan.

It is easier to guide and correct children while they are young because you are building them up, but be careful of what you are putting into them by what you say and do in front of them. It is harder to correct them as they become older. It is a good thing to teach them how to live productive lives and be good citizens, but the best thing to impart is the Word of God. We must then teach them how to apply God's Word in their daily lives so they can live lives that are pleasing to God.

*In whatever areas we neglect to teach our children, the Devil will seek to take advantage of those opportunities to push our children away from God and away from us as parents.

*The things that are important to God should be important to us, and we should impart them unto our beloved children, for they are "Tomorrow's Church." We are to pass on the faith of the Lord Jesus Christ.

"To desire that ye might be filled with the knowledge of his will in all wisdom and spiritual understanding: That ye might walk worthy of the Lord unto all pleasing, being fruitful in every good work, and increasing in the knowledge of God." (Colossians 1:9b-10)

The Bible has everything needed for individuals to have a successful Christian life and a good Christian family, but we will succeed only if we are seeking God and obeying what He instructs us to do. This applies to raising our children, managing our finances and relationships, living holy lives, dealing with the loss of loved ones, and much more. 2 Timothy 3:16-17 states, "All scripture is given by inspiration of God, and is profitable for doctrine, for reproof, for correction, for instruction in righteousness: That the man of God may be perfect, throughly furnished unto all good works."

God's Word instructs us how to handle the situations we face in this life in such a way that we can bring honor and glory unto God. By doing so, we will also benefit because we have a great God that rewards His children's obedience. I also recognize that we need to have the right motives in serving the Lord. One can do all the things that are right in the sight of God and still fail to please God if the motives of his heart are wrong. The Bible says in Matthew 6:33, "But seek ye first the kingdom of God, and his righteousness; and all these things shall be added unto you."

Another example that comes to mind is the church of Ephesus in Revelation 2:1-7. This church did everything right, but God had a problem with the church because they had left their first love

(Revelation 2:4-5). It is possible to attempt to raise our children for the Lord and use the correct methods, yet not achieve the desired goal because we have excluded God.

---

*God should be at the center of our lives, and everything else built around God.

Hebrews 11:6 says, "But without faith it is impossible to please him, for he that cometh to God must believe that he is, and that he is a rewarder of them that diligently seek him." Think about the reward for obedience: God wants to bless His people.

The Bible says in Psalm 1:2, "But **his delight is in the law of the LORD**; and in his law doth he meditate day and night." Think about your motives, the reasons why you do what you do for God. There should be a desire to seek the Lord and learn about Him and learn more from Him.

By obeying God, you and I can obtain a good testimony before others, but especially in the sight of our beloved children. With that testimony, you and I can be good witnesses for the Lord and have the opportunity to lead people to God through salvation. If you already know God as your Savior, by your testimony you can encourage others to develop a stronger relationship with God.

We need to be aware that our testimony is how we conduct ourselves, meaning how we communicate both verbally and through our actions with others. The Bible says in Matthew 5:14-16, "Ye are the light of the world. A city that is set on an hill cannot be hid. Neither do men light a candle, and put it under a bushel, but on a candlestick; and it giveth light unto all that are in the house. Let your light so shine before men, that they may see your good works, and glorify your Father which is in heaven."

I believe that it should be the desire of Christian parents to see their children get saved and walk with the Lord. One of the methods that

God will use to influence them is the life of their parents. But in order for parents' testimonies to be effective in this matter, they have to live their faith consistently in and out of the house.

Christian parents should be witnesses for the Lord. Proverbs 11:30 says, "The fruit of the righteous is a tree of life; and he that winneth souls is wise." The Bible also states in James 5:20, "Let him know, that he which converteth the sinner from the error of his way shall save a soul from death, and shall hide a multitude of sins." In order for us to be effective Christians and have the ability to influence others (especially those in our own homes), we must consistently be living out our faith in the Lord Jesus Christ. **"We cannot be Christians in name only"**.

The Bible has all that we need for everything you and I will face; and, most importantly, the Bible is the final authority. You may be wondering why I talked about a person's testimony, soul winning (sharing the gospel), living right, obeying God, and more. After all, this is a book about raising children. **I mentioned all of that because they are all related.**

How we live our lives before others speaks volumes about what we believe and about the God we serve. Our children see and know about God first by what we say and do! I have made this statement for many years to the parents of the children I worked with at the child development center:

"Children learn by what we say, what we do, and what we don't correct." In light of that statement, we as parents need to recognize the God-given authority and influence we have in our children's lives. They are watching your every move in life, they are listening to your every word, they are observing your every choice. What is your life teaching them?

The Bible says in Proverbs 22:6, "Train up a child in the way he should go: and when he is old, he will not depart from it." The Bible also says in Ephesians 6:4, "And, ye fathers, provoke not your children to wrath: **but bring them up in the nurture and admonition of the Lord.**" As parents, we teach our children through our verbal and non-verbal testimony—by what we say and do. As Christian parents, we should be teaching them and instructing them daily. I am reminded of when God brought His people out of Egyptian bondage and commanded them to teach their children about Him and tell them what He had done for them: "And thou **shalt teach them diligently unto thy children, and shalt talk of them when thou sittest in thine house, and when thou walkest by the way, and when thou liest down, and when thou risest up. And thou shalt bind them for a sign upon thine hand, and they shall be as frontlets between thine eyes. And thou shalt write them upon the posts of thy house, and on thy gates**" (Deuteronomy 6:7-9).

God impressed upon my heart through these verses that we as parents should be teaching the Word of God to our children and showing them how to apply the Word of God to their lives. Not only that, but we should also be sharing our testimony with our children about how God has answered our prayers and how God is working in our lives. It will encourage them to realize that God is real and that He desires to be there for us and to answer our prayers, if we are living right according to His will. It will also remind them not to forget God.

"God has unconditional love for us, but He has conditional promises."

To put it simply, if you and I will be obedient to Him, God will fulfill His promises to us as we live for Him.

For example, if my children are obeying me and consistently following what I have taught and instructed them to do (they are doing what is right), I find that they can come to me and ask me for things. Depending on what it is, I may give it to them, and sometimes I will even do special things for them or surprise them with a gift because of their good behavior. But if they are not doing right and they ask me for things, most likely they won't receive it from me! Why? Because our fellowship is not right because of their conduct—because they did what is wrong in my sight. It is the same with God toward us.

Read and truly listen to this scripture: "The just man walketh in his integrity: his children are blessed after him" (Proverbs 20:7).

"Don't underestimate your influence as a parent. A parent can mold character and point a son or daughter in the right or wrong direction in life!"

Purpose of Dedicating
Your Children unto the Lord

Truly think about what you are saying when you choose to dedicate your children unto the Lord. It is a life-long commitment unto God. We as parents must be consistent and faithful in this matter and know that God will help us to fulfill our promise of raising our children for Him. Also, recognize that God has already equipped you to do so by providing His Word to instruct you and His Spirit to comfort and guide you. *God wants you to succeed!*

Dedicating our children to the Lord is a promise that Christian parents make to the Lord to raise, teach, and encourage their child (or children) to know the Lord personally and to live for God.

It is a promise to turn away from religious and family traditions and raise their children in the truth of God's word. Paul admonishes us in Colossians 2:8, "Beware lest any man spoil you through philosophy and vain deceit, after the tradition of men, after the rudiments of the world, and not after Christ." These parents promise to live consistently for the Lord, attempting to set a good Christian example before their children.

These parents say unto God that His ways are right, that His ways are perfect, and that they will raise their children using the Word of God as the final and only authority. We acknowledge that the Bible holds the answers for every area of our lives, and we will seek God for the answers that we need.

We need to teach our children, but in order for us to be teachers we need to sit under and learn from the Great Teacher (God) and ask Him to give us knowledge, wisdom, and discernment. The Bible says in James 1:5, "If any of you lack wisdom, let him ask of God, that giveth to all men liberally, and upbraideth not; and it shall be given him." The Bible lets us know that, if we ask for it, it will be given. In Matthew 7:7, Christ says, "Ask, and it shall be given you; seek, and ye shall find; knock, and it shall be opened unto you." Matthew 21:22 continues, "And all things, whatsoever ye shall ask in prayer, believing, ye shall receive." When we pray in line with the will of God, God will answer our prayers, and it is His will for us to teach and raise our children that they may know Him and live for Him.

Acts 2:38-39 says, "Then Peter said unto them, Repent, and be baptized every one of you in the name of Jesus Christ for the remission of sins, and ye shall receive the gift of the Holy Ghost. For the promise is unto you, and to your children, and to all that are afar off, even as many as the Lord our God shall call." *We need to recognize that it is God's will and desire for Christians to be successful in raising their children.*

Conducting Devotions
with Your Children

In Deuteronomy 6:7 and 11:19, God instructs us to take hold of opportunities to teach our children about Him and to share testimonies of what God has done in our lives. In Proverbs 22:6, God lets us know that we need to train up our children and that whatever we instill in them will remain in them, whether it be good or bad, for God or not. In Ephesians 6:4, God instructs fathers not to provoke their children to wrath, but rather to bring them up by nurturing them and pointing them towards the Lord. In these scriptures and many others, God impressed upon my heart the importance of family devotionals and the responsibility of parents to teach their children about God. It is the parents' job to encourage their children to seek the Lord by teaching them the Word of God and showing them how to apply it to their lives.

Parents are the primary ones that should be teaching their children about the Lord and the things of God. Churches and Christian schools should be secondary and should reinforce what has and is being taught at home. **The home is where the foundations for life should be set first; everything else should reinforce your teachings.**

Family devotions in the home are vital. We have a small window of opportunity in which to influence our children's lives for the Lord. **Parents need to take hold of the opportunity to teach their children the Word of God, prayerfully teaching them in a way that shows them how to apply the Bible in their day-to-day lives.** Parents must teach them Bible doctrine, showing them from the Scriptures how to deal with various situations they are facing or may face, such as low self-esteem, bullying, praying unto the Lord, or treating other people the way that God wants them to be treated. We must teach them how to conduct themselves socially, morally, and professionally, instructing them from the Bible on how to be good siblings, how to be good parents, how to trust God, as well as how and why they should share the gospel. The Bible is truly a manual for life!

Scripture support (Teaching and pointing our children unto the Lord): "And, ye fathers, provoke not your children to wrath: but bring them up in the nurture and admonition of the Lord." (Ephesians 6:4)

Scripture support (Soul winning): "The fruit of the righteous is a tree of life; and he that winneth souls is wise." (Proverbs 11:30)

Scripture support (Soul winning): "Brethren, if any of you do err from the truth, and one convert him; Let him know, that he which converteth the sinner from the error of his way shall save a soul from death, and shall hide a multitude of sins." (James 5:19-20)

Scripture support (Treatment of others): "Therefore all things whatsoever ye would that men should do to you, do ye even so to them: for this is the law and the prophets." (Matthew 7:12) "And as ye would that men should do to you, do ye also to them likewise." (Luke 6:31)

Scripture support (Developing a good relationship): "Iron sharpeneth iron; so a man sharpeneth the countenance of his friend." (Proverbs 27:17) "A man that hath friends must shew himself friendly: and there is a friend that sticketh closer than a brother." (Proverbs 18:24)

Scripture support: "This book of the law shall not depart out of thy mouth; but thou shalt meditate therein day and night, that thou mayest observe to do according to all that is written therein: for then thou shalt make thy way prosperous, and then thou shalt have good success." (Joshua 1:8) "Study to shew thyself approved unto God, a workman that needeth not to be ashamed, rightly dividing the word of truth." (2 Timothy 2:15)

Below are some tips that can help you when conducting your devotionals:

Tip #1: In our devotionals with our families, we should attempt to engage our children by having them read some of the Scriptures within the lessons if they are able. I encourage the teacher of the devotional to ask them questions about the lesson to see if they are understanding and paying attention to the lesson. (I also suggest asking your children some questions while the lesson is in progress, as well as after the lesson.) When you ask them what the lesson was about, don't worry if they come up with some thoughts that you didn't teach them directly, but make sure what they say to you lines up in some manner with the lesson that was taught. I find that God may speak to our hearts in a particular way for what we need to hear. It is similar to church services where everyone takes away something different from the sermon that was preached, because God will speak to our hearts differently. We face different things in our walk of faith, and we all are at different levels of spiritual maturity. Praise God that He will speak to us! And when you ask your children what the lesson was about, it is good to allow them to express it in their own words; that will show you if they understand what was taught to them.

Tip #2: Sometimes when I read our Bible text aloud, I will read, then stop and give my children the opportunity to pick up where I left off reading. I find that it helps them to stay focused on our lesson. It allows them the opportunity to be a part of the lesson, engaging them. It also gives them the chance to get comfortable and gain confidence with reading out loud and speaking in front of other people. I find that it makes them pay close attention to the Scripture reading, because they don't know at times when I am going to stop reading and when they will have to continue reading. There are other times when I will assign reading so that they know when it is their turn.

Tip #3: If you have an older child who is saved and is growing in spiritual maturity, I encourage you to allow them to prayerfully construct a devotional to teach to the family. It will encourage them to seek God and allow God to work in their hearts. I have found that my son was joyful that He had heard from God, and his confidence and faith in the Lord grew.

Tip #4: "And ye shall teach them your children, speaking of them when thou sittest in thine house, and when thou walkest by the way, when thou liest down, and when thou risest up." (Deuteronomy 11:19)

Teaching our children about the Lord should not be confined to our homes or to the church alone; we should be teaching our beloved children about God using every opportunity, regardless of the environment. The Bible says in Deuteronomy 6:7, "And thou shalt teach them diligently unto thy children, and shalt talk of them when thou sittest in thine house, and when thou walkest by the way, and when thou liest down, and when thou risest up."

Every moment in life can be a teachable moment.

We can use the things and people that we see around us as we walk with our children, drive in the car with our children, sit somewhere with them, and more. It is important to explain to them what is right and wrong in the sight of God and teach them how they need to live their lives in a manner that pleases God, helping them to see that God will honor and reward His people for their faithfulness unto Him. Bring to light in their hearts how much God loves everyone but hates sin, and share with them the importance of reaching people with the gospel.

Tip #5: Devotionals do not have to be very long. You do not have to preach a sermon to your family; just express clearly what God wants you to say. Remember, just like we went to school daily to be educated, we need to be consistent in teaching our children, grandchildren, and youth in general the Word of God.

"Chasten thy son while there is hope, and let not thy soul spare for his crying." (Proverbs 19:18)

We as parents need to guide our children in the right direction while we still have influence and ability because, once that moment of opportunity is gone, that is it! Think about that statement from the scripture above, "Chasten thy son while there is hope." Guide your children, invest your life in them for God while they are under your care, because soon they will be adults living apart from you and what you have put into them will come out.

Regardless of what the world teaches, we know that the greatest teachers to our children are their parents. Parents are the first and most important influences in a child's life. A parent's words and actions can destroy a child or build them up!

Tip #6: Encourage your children to spend time with the Lord in prayer and in studying and reading their Bible. Set up a daily routine. I encourage my children to seek the Lord in the morning and evening through their own personal prayer and Bible time.

An example of our schedule: 1) Prayer and Bible reading in the morning. 2) Afternoon Bible reading. (Depending on time because of homework. This portion of the schedule works better during the summer.)

3) Prayer and Bible reading before bed. (I also encourage them to pray to God throughout the course of the day and I have explained to my beloved children that **"prayer is our communication with God."** I tell my children that prayer does not have to be long; it can be taking a moment to thank the Lord, to praise Him, or even to ask for His help.)

I shared with my children this single thought: "Would you like it if someone that you love would not talk to you or spend time with you?" They replied back to me that, no, they wouldn't like it! I told them that is possibly how God might feel about us when we do not take the time to seek Him in prayer or to read and study His Word. I informed them that we are sinning against God when we choose not to pray and read the Word of God, because God commands us to pray consistently. An example of this is found in 1 Thessalonians 5:17: "Pray without ceasing." We obey God when we pray unto Him. Other Scriptures that talk about prayer are Philippians 4:6, Ephesians 6:18, 1 Timothy 2:1, Colossians 4:2, Romans 12:12, Luke 18:1, and Matthew 26:41.

God wants us to study and read the Bible. This is found in 2 Timothy 2:15: "Study to shew thyself approved unto God, a workman that needeth not to be ashamed, rightly dividing the word of truth." God does not say to read His Word or pray when we feel like it. No, He tells us in these verses, as well as in other places, that we need to pray, read, and study the Bible.

Tip #7: There are some parents that may find it difficult to arrange some time within their daily schedules to sit down and have a family devotion. Is there anything within your schedule that you could remove or cut down? I ask a foolish but powerful question: "What is more important to you: your children and their development, or your personal time?" Remember that you have a short time to influence your children. Children, when they are grown, can bring great joy or frustration and pain, depending on how they live their lives.

Consider these passages:

- Proverbs 29:17 – "Correct thy son, and he shall give thee rest; yea, he shall give delight unto thy soul."
- Proverbs 29:15 – "The rod and reproof give wisdom: but a child left to himself bringeth his mother to shame."
- Proverbs 10:1 – "The proverbs of Solomon. A wise son maketh a glad father: but a foolish son is the heaviness of his mother."
- Proverbs 17:21 – "He that begetteth a fool doeth it to his sorrow: and the father of a fool hath no joy."

The time that you invest now may be the difference between having a foolish child or having a wise child that brings honor and glory unto God and your family.

"Not everything you do in life is going to be easy, but the things we struggle with tend to yield the most rewards in our lives". *For example, the things that we struggle within our faith, God uses to strengthen us and to mold our character, and through that very struggle we learn how to trust God. We are able to see Him work in our lives through answered prayer and needs met, and so much more!*

Teaching Your Children
How to Select Friends

Teaching your children how to select friends is important because who you spend time with does affect your behavior over time, and the effects of those influences can be subtle or dramatic. We, as parents, need to teach our children from God's Word how to select their friends and how to protect themselves from poisonous relationships. We should also teach them how to be good friends.

The Bible says in 1 Corinthians 15:33, "Be not deceived: evil communications corrupt good manners."

It would be practically impossible for anyone to shield their children from all of the individuals that could negatively influence them, but we can teach our children godly principles to apply that will help to keep them from poisonous relationships. It will help them to identify good friends and learn how they can be good friends themselves.

Another reason it is important to teach our children about this matter of friendship is that sometimes children are attracted to the wrong influences in their lives. In fact, they seem to gravitate towards those individuals or people that are not good influences on them.

We need to use the Bible to instruct our children on the importance of friendship.

The Bible says in 1 Corinthians 15:33, "Be not deceived." The word *deceived* in the scriptural text means (1) to roam from safety, from truth; (2) to go astray; (3) to err, be seduced, wander; (4) to be out of the way. The first portion of Scripture lets us know that there is the possibility of a person being seduced by ungodly influences in such a way that they may willfully turn away from the truth and abandon the principles, morals, and teachings they were taught in their youth. And if they do not abandon their upbringing, they may compromise their personal beliefs and righteous standards in order to fellowship with that individual or group of people.

The latter part of that Scripture says, "Evil communications corrupt good manners." This portion of Scripture lets us know that, over time, a person's good manners or good moral habits can be corrupted. The degree of that corruption depends on the strength of that person. In light of this truth, we need to be serious about this matter of teaching our children how to select friends and how to distinguish between good and bad relationships.

Think about how we may search for a friend. We may consciously or subconsciously select a friend by what we find attractive about that individual, such as common interests (for example, we both enjoy reading, have a similar fashion sense, etc.) or the need for long-term or short-term companionship. Sometimes I have noticed young people developing friendships with individuals that are negative influences in their life because they were not taught a method for choosing a friend. Below are some rules I gave my children to help them:

Rule #1: Good friends care for one another.

"A friend loveth at all times, and a brother is born for adversity" (Proverbs 17:17). A friend is concerned for you because they care about you. A good friend will support you, encourage you, and be there for you in the hard times.

Rule #2: Good friends will point you in the right direction and tell you when you are wrong.

"Faithful are the wounds of a friend; but the kisses of an enemy are deceitful" (Proverbs 27:6). A good friend is trustworthy, honest, and truthful with you no matter the cost; they will tell you the truth about certain matters, even if that truth may hurt you. They will support you in the things that are right and good, they will not encourage you to do what is wrong, and they will have a heart to advise you in a good and godly course of action.

Rule #3: Let go of poisonous relationships and work to hold on to a good friendship.

"Thine own friend, and thy father's friend, forsake not; neither go into thy brother's house in the day of thy calamity: for better is a neighbour that is near than a brother far off" (Proverbs 27:10). For this text of Scripture, we are going to focus on the first portion which says, "Thine own friend, and thy father's friend, forsake not." There are going to be times in our lives that we will have to separate ourselves from certain friends because our relationship with them is pulling us toward the wrong direction. But this Scripture tells us that we should not forsake a friend; we should not turn our backs on a good friend, without just cause.

Rule #4: Good friends sharpen one another.

"Iron sharpeneth iron; so a man sharpeneth the countenance of his friend" (Proverbs 27:17). Good friends will encourage one another in doing what is right, help one another to remain honest, develop one another's esteem and good character, and hold each other accountable. In essence, by their unique differences, God can use them to edify one another.

Rule #5: Treat a friend how you want to be treated.

"A man that hath friends must shew himself friendly: and there is a friend that sticketh closer than a brother" (Proverbs 18:24). A good friend must show himself to be friendly. He must display warmth, hospitality, and respect, treating his friend how he would want to be treated. The Bible says in Luke 6:31, "And as ye would that men should do to you, do ye also to them likewise" (see also Matthew 7:12).

Rule #6: A good friend supports you when you are right, and when you are doing what is right.

The Bible says in Ecclesiastes 4:9-10, "Two are better than one; because they have a good reward for their labour. For if they fall, the one will lift up his fellow: but woe to him that is alone when he falleth: for he hath not another to help him up." They will be faithful to support one another and provide a helping hand when one is in need. We all need help in this life, whether we choose to realize it or not. There are times when the burden we carry is too heavy and we need a friend to help lighten the load. It is good to have some people that you can walk with in life.

The company we keep will affect us, and that is why it is important for us to surround ourselves with people that will have a godly impact on our lives. That influence is not one-sided; we also need to be ones that affect others.

Listening to Our Children

The Bible says in James 1:19, "Wherefore, my beloved brethren, let every man be swift to hear, slow to speak, slow to wrath." God wants us to be quick to listen, slow to speak and slow to wrath. I find that, depending on the situation we are in, this can be rather difficult to do, but with God's help all things are possible (Matthew 19:26). One of the hardest things for a person to do is to listen silently to someone. I believe it can be difficult because we are all selfish creatures by nature. We want to be heard, we want to be seen, we desire the attention of others. Some people desire attention more than others, but we all desire it to some degree. I have especially noticed this in children. There is nothing wrong with needing attention as long as it is done in a healthy and constructive manner.

Our children need to be heard, and they need their parents to pay attention to them. We, as parents, need to let our children know that we are available to them and that they have access to us. We must be willing to make time for them, listen to them and give them the liberty to share their heart respectfully with us. **I encourage parents not to be their children's friend, but rather to be their parent first and then a friend.** Your children should be able to come and talk with you openly, yet respect the authority you have over them. Often, I have witnessed, when parents attempt to be their children's friend, that their children have little or no respect for their parent's authority. We need to understand that friends are equals, and therefore they can talk to one another any way they choose. **I encourage you to operate in the authority that God has given you over your children, so you can effectively guide them in the right direction. Remember, when you build the right relationship with your children the door of communication and fellowship will always be open between you and them.**

The Bible says in Luke 11:9, "And I say unto you, Ask, and it shall be given you; seek, and ye shall find; knock, and it shall be opened unto you."

Matthew 11:28 says, "Come unto me, all ye that labour and are heavy laden, and I will give you rest."

God, as our Heavenly Father, invites us to speak with Him and to fellowship with Him. He wants us to communicate with Him, expressing the burdens and cares of our hearts. He lets us know that we have access to Him at all times through prayer.

We need to let our children know that this is the same message we have for them concerning communication with us. We need to inform our children that they have access to come to us anytime to communicate and fellowship with us because we love them and desire to be there for them.

It is our responsibility as parents to express to our children that we are available to them for counsel and conversation. We should be available to listen to them, allowing our children to express respectfully and truthfully what is on their heart. I tell my children, **"You can always talk with me about anything, and even though I may not like what you tell me, I am always here for you."**

I have found that, by applying God's principles in this matter, my beloved children have come to talk to me about deeply personal matters of the heart. Because of that, I have been able to guide them through the stages of their lives and, at times, even away from sinful choices.

We need to take the time to listen to our children. We need to allow them the opportunity to completely express their thoughts, whether we like them or not, as long as it is expressed respectfully. That demonstrates to our children that we are someone that they can turn to and that we will listen to them; by doing so, we also demonstrate how they should interact with others. By doing this, we can strengthen our bond with our beloved children.

Because we are human, it is sometimes necessary to let them know that you need a break from communicating with them. I recall moments when my children would "unload the truck" and tell me so many things that I would have to express to them that I needed a break from the conversation, and later we will pick up where we left off. Make sure you get back to them to continue that conversation. God takes time to listen to us completely, and we (though imperfect) should attempt to model ourselves after the example of the Lord.

Consider these Scripture passages:

- James 1:19 – "Wherefore, my beloved brethren, let every man be swift to hear, slow to speak, slow to wrath."

- 1 Peter 2:21 – "For even hereunto were ye called: because Christ also suffered for us, leaving us an example, that ye should follow his steps."

- 1 John 2:4-6 – "He that saith, I know him, and keepeth not his commandments, is a liar, and the truth is not in him. But whoso keepeth his word, in him verily is the love of God perfected: hereby know we that we are in him. He that saith he abideth in him ought himself also so to walk, even as he walked."

We need to follow God's example to us and God's instruction for us. In like manner, we need to model the appropriate behavior so that our children can see what good communication looks like and emulate our example.

Whatever we teach our children to do, we should model the very thing we are attempting to instill in them. We cannot have a philosophy of "do as I say and not as I do"! We are not perfect, but our words and actions need to consistently match.

Not only should we listen to our children, but we also need to make ourselves available to our children or to the young people that are in our care. We can make ourselves available by letting them know that we can be trusted by meeting their needs as well as some of their wants. (Please don't confuse needs and wants: needs are the essentials things, and wants are just the desires of the child. Some wants are good, but not all wants should be met.)

We need to make ourselves available just like God makes Himself available unto us. The Bible says in James 4:8, "Draw nigh to God, and he will draw nigh to you. Cleanse your hands, ye sinners; and purify your hearts, ye double minded."

When you have established a good foundation, your children will be able to discuss deeper things. They will talk with you about personal topics that many are uncomfortable discussing, such as sex, the changes going on with their bodies, relationships, attraction to others, their response to that attraction, dealing with loss, and a variety of other things. Good lines of communication can strengthen the bonds between a parent and child.

*Food for Thought:

"How our children deal with others is in direct relationship to how we as parents treat them!"

Tips on Disciplining

I shared with my children this thought about listening and obedience: **"Good listening is doing what you are told when you are told to do it, and not when you get ready to."** Many times, I observe parents telling their children to do something, and that child may perform it, but they do it slowly and with a nasty attitude. That negative behavior must be stopped. Good biblical discipline will aid in weeding out negative attitudes from your child. Parents need to role-model and teach them what is appropriate and what is not.

A pyramid is widest at the bottom and narrowest at the top. A pyramid is a picture of how biblical discipline should affect our children's lives as we apply it. As we set a Biblical foundation of discipline, like a pyramid, the most discipline should occur when our children are very young (represented by the widest part of the pyramid), and as they grow older we should have to correct them less because we have taught them how to obey (represented by the narrowest section of the pyramid). Biblical discipline is instructing, training, teaching, and also applying physical corrections to our children. God's method for raising our children should be applied consistently and should be the only method we use. We cannot get godly results mixing God's way with the world's way ("world" meaning your own philosophies, cultural philosophies of the world concerning child rearing, or your parents' methods if it differs from God's ways).

*If it doesn't line up with God's Word, then we should not to do it.

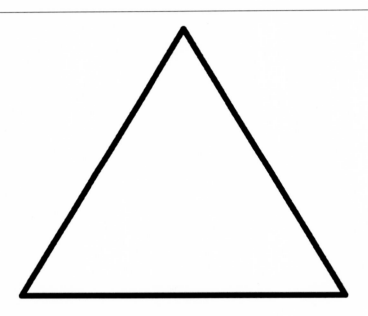

God is not the author of confusion; He is a God of order and balance. The Bible says in 1 Corinthians 14:33, "For God is not the author of confusion, but of peace, as in all churches of the saints."

God also impressed upon my heart the illustration of a circle. A circle is balanced; there is not one area higher or lower than the other side. Let that circle represent our love, instruction, discipline, teaching, consistency and correction, and being a godly role model to our children.

With God's formula properly applied, our children can be balanced. We will see more positive behavior and an increase in obedience from a sincere heart. Respect towards parents and other good traits will emerge. We will notice less challenging behavior as they get older. We must stay with God's way and **not mix or add our philosophies in raising our children.** Many times, throughout my career as a teacher/caregiver, I have observed parents being imbalanced in how they are raising their children. They were too strong in one or two areas, weak in some areas, or negligent in other areas. For example, I knew a parent that was strong in correction and discipline but weak in showing love, in teaching, and in communication to others in their family (talking, listening to each other, and then responding to the situation). If you and I are not careful, we can build the wrong type of foundation in our children, causing more difficulties in their life and also in our lives because of what we did or did not do!

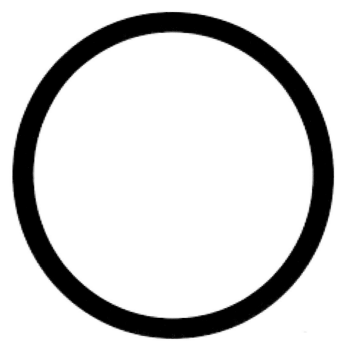

God's ways work when you do it! We cannot combine the world's philosophies with God's and expect

> **godly results. It is like oil and water—they do not mix.**

*If you and I can trust God to save us, why can we not trust and obey what the Bible tells us to do concerning raising our children. Remember, God knows best! The Bible says in Proverbs 3:5-6, "Trust in the LORD with all thine heart; and lean not unto thine own understanding. In all thy ways acknowledge him, <u>and he shall direct thy paths</u>."

The Difference between Character and Negative Behavior

We need to understand that there is a difference between character and negative behavior (being disobedient). An individual can be strong-willed and obedient, or a child can be shy and obedient. **But no matter the character type, that individual can learn to be obedient to positive authority.** Our society teaches the opposite. It teaches that character solely dictates the behavior of an individual and that the negative behavior sometimes cannot be changed because it is the result of the individual's character. **That type of philosophy is false.**

The Bible says in Proverbs 22:15, "Foolishness is bound in the heart of a child; but the rod of correction shall drive it far from him." God's discipline will allow you to weed out and uproot negative behavior and character that can cause problems (for example, lying, stealing, boasting, being conceited, and bullying). You and I need to obey God in raising our children. We need to understand that it is a combination of teaching, training, and instruction, along with physical correction. All of these components become effective when they are used together.

We, as parents, need to set the right foundation, teaching our children to be obedient early. The later you wait to provide good, godly discipline, the harder it will be to guide them out of that negative behavior as they get older. The Bible says in Proverbs 19:18, "Chasten thy son while there is hope, and let not thy soul spare for his crying." There will be a point when you may not have much influence over your children; you need to start guiding them early.

When you correct your children God's way, you will find that your children will bring you joy in the way they conduct themselves in (and out) of your presence. The Bible says in Proverbs 29:17, "Correct thy son, and he shall give thee rest; yea, he shall give delight unto thy soul."

Let us think about proper physical discipline: it is one of the key components in raising and encouraging our children to do what is right! The Bible says in Proverbs 13:24, "He that spareth his rod hateth his son: but he that loveth him chasteneth him betimes." (*Betimes* means "early.") We love our children. I believe the majority of parents would say that, but is it love when you allow your children to behave in a destructive manner? Love is having the courage to correct someone who is heading in the wrong direction. Think of the wonderful example of Christ when He took our place at Calvary. Because I love my children, I am going to correct negative behavior, especially realizing that, if I do not correct that behavior now while I have the ability and opportunity, it will be my fault when they become adults that struggle in those same areas.

We as Christians need to realize that we will be held accountable to God for the things we do and do not do! The Bible says in Romans 14:11-12, "For it is written, As I live, saith the Lord, every knee shall bow to me, and every tongue shall confess to God. So then every one of us shall give account of himself to God." And the Bible says in Matthew 12:35-37, "A good man out of the good treasure of the heart bringeth forth good things: and an evil man out of the evil treasure bringeth forth evil things. But I say unto you, That every idle word that men shall speak, they shall give account thereof in the day of judgment. For by thy words thou shalt be justified, and by thy words thou shalt be condemned." Every Christian and every sinner will be held accountable before God. For that reason, and because of the love God has for us, that should motivate us to want to correct our children the right way, God's way!

*Physical Discipline: This topic has caused controversy and division among many people, including married couples. Should parents physically discipline their children? What is the proper way to physically discipline your children? Some people suggest that, when you physically correct your child, you are abusing them. (That is a person that has not seen nor experienced proper discipline themselves.) In my experiences as a caregiver/teacher, I have noticed that the majority of parents that adopt a philosophy of non-physical discipline use systems of bribery and timeout to get their children to do what they want and need them to do. I have also noticed the consistent frustration they experience as they attempt to get their children to listen and to obey their commands and instructions. It seems that many of the children brought up using those techniques frequently repeat the behaviors that the parent is attempting to correct. There are plenty of examples I could present to you, but many have one thing in common: they struggle frequently, and it is harder to correct negative behavior concerning their children.

God, the creator of mankind, knows how we should be raised. God knows what is best in order to produce a good, godly person. The Bible says in Proverbs 22:15, "Foolishness is bound in the heart of a child; but the rod of correction shall drive it far from him." Understand that physical discipline is not an instrument of cruelty or abuse. It is a tool that God gives a parent to effectively deal with a child's negative behavior in order to encourage them to do what is right and to learn to obey parental authority. (**Obedience brings harmony within a family**.)

I have witnessed many families that struggle greatly with disobedient children. They are frustrated, and there is chaos both in the home and whenever they take the children into different environments. I have also seen the opposite: when children are obedient, there is peace within that home and wherever they go. People are glad that they are around.

Once again, godly physical discipline is a tool that God gives a parent to effectively deal with a child's negative behavior in order to encourage them to do what is right and to learn to obey parental authority. I find that when physical discipline is applied correctly to our children, that issues are not often repeated. Discipline should be done in a loving manner, not when an individual is extremely upset. (Know that there is nothing wrong with being disappointed with your child's conduct.) You have to prayerfully decide how much pressure to apply, but it should be done in a manner that your child would not want that discipline to occur again. Your discipline should be done consistently and in a way that encourages your child to obey and to choose to do what is right in and out of your presence.

Proverbs 23:12-14 says, "Apply thine heart unto instruction, and thine ears to the words of knowledge. Withhold not correction from the child: for if thou beatest him with the rod, he shall not die. Thou shalt beat him with the rod, and shalt deliver his soul from hell." Godly discipline is not abuse; godly correction will affect our children in a positive manner if done the right way. Godly correction, instruction, teaching, and discipline will build up our children, encouraging them to communicate and conduct themselves in a way that pleases and glorifies God.

In our society today, parents use physical discipline as a last result or not at all. As a teacher/caregiver for about 14 years, I have observed how frustrated parents are with the negative behavior that the child exhibits. (Also, think of the frustration that caregivers experience attempting to deal with these children on a regular basis. I have personally worked with children that hit, spit, verbally disrespect adults, destroy the property around them, and hurt or attempt to hurt their peers physically and verbally. I recall parents getting upset with caregivers for talking with them about their child's behavior.

A caregiver is simply dealing with the behavior that the parent has allowed to develop.) God's ways of discipline, if done consistently and correctly, will encourage positive behavior. Remember that God holds us accountable for what we know, say, and do, and we as parents need to follow God's example and raise our children accordingly. If I have taught my children something or instructed them to do something, then they will be held accountable for not doing it, and punishment will come immediately if it is not followed. As for the amount of physical discipline you give your children; you need to allow God to guide you, but it should be done in a way that encourages them to do right and that discourages them from repeating their poor choice again because they are aware of the consequences. (I encourage parents to pray before correcting their children. That will help you get into the right frame of mind, especially if you are upset because of your child's conduct.)

Obedience brings harmony; the opposite is true too. When you have children that behave poorly, it affects others around them. I have observed children that behave poorly, physically harming their peers and verbally abusing their peers. I have also seen in classroom settings, when those children are not around, that the attitude of the room is relaxed and calm for the other children as well as for the teacher/caregiver. When children are disciplined God's way and taught and instructed in the things of righteousness, there will be harmony and peace in their environment.

Just because you may be physically disciplining your children does not mean that you are doing it correctly or in the manner that God has instructed. Some parents are doing one part of what God tells us to do in reference to raising our children. You and I will not get godly results by doing some of what God says for us to do! We must do it all.

> ***Discipline + instruction + teaching + leading by example + praying for our children + physical correction = true godly results**.

You will face some challenges as you apply God's principles, but know that they can be overcome by consistently obeying what God tells you to do! There will be exterior and interior influences that your child will encounter. Because we are all sinners, we are born with a sin nature. The Bible says in Romans 5:12, "Wherefore, as by one man sin entered into the world, and death by sin; and so death passed upon all men, for that all have sinned." Children are not born doing right; they have to be taught to do right!

With my eldest son, we went through more struggles concerning his negative behavior with others. I had to teach him to respect positive authority as long as they are telling him to do what is right. (Not all authorities around our children are good ones!)

I recall him getting into trouble at elementary school, and for a period of time I had to discipline him weekly (and sometimes daily), but I never doubted God's methods. I was consistent in God's method of punishment, and soon there was a positive change. (The end result was what God promised.) Both of my children have a good testimony at school among teachers and peers as Christians with good moral character.

Proper Child Discipline:

God has designed physical discipline for parents as a way to guide, encourage, and teach their children. When you physically discipline your children, know that you should use it as a tool to teach them. They should be held accountable for the **"knowledge they have"**, and the instructions they have disobeyed; then godly correction should follow. **"Proper godly discipline does not cause negative effects, but rather the opposite"**.

Pointing Our Children
in the Direction of the Lord

"And, ye fathers, provoke not your children to wrath: but bring them up in the nurture and admonition of the Lord." (Ephesians 6:4)

Parents are commanded to bring up their children for the Lord, teaching them, disciplining them, instructing them in the ways of God. We should be encouraging them through our daily testimony and teaching them practical application of the Word of God through Bible lessons at home and by taking advantage of teachable moments throughout the day.

Every day is filled with teachable moments—opportunities that can be used to teach your children various truths that will equip and enrich them. These truths will also prepare them for the future, giving them the tools they need to succeed so they can stand on their own and fulfill the will of God for their life.

We need to keep in mind that we will have our children for a short period of time. We must raise them to stand on their own and to live right.

I heard this statement years ago: "A teacher is there to teach the student so that the student no longer will need the teacher." I recall sharing this thought with many of the families I have worked with through the years: "A parent's job is to equip their children so they can stand, with and without us." We should build them up, so they can be adults that honor God and their families.

The Bible says in Proverbs 23:24-25, "The father of the righteous shall greatly rejoice: and he that begetteth a wise child shall have joy of him. Thy father and thy mother shall be glad, and she that bare thee shall rejoice." I believe it is the desire of the majority of parents to see their children live in such a way that they can greatly rejoice because of their conduct. We will be pleased, but, most importantly, God is pleased when His children are living according to His perfect will. God promises that what we impart to them will not fade away. The Bible says in Proverbs 22:6, "Train up a child in the way he should go: and when he is old, he will not depart from it." We need to remember that it is our responsibility to raise them for the Lord, not just to raise them to be good citizens.

As we raise our children we should not provoke them to wrath, but we should nurture them. I have seen parents cause their children to despise them and rebel against their teachings because they treat them in a disparaging manner. The Bible says in Ephesians 6:4, "And, ye fathers, provoke not your children to wrath: but bring them up in the nurture and admonition of the Lord." The heaviest weight falls upon the father's shoulders, but the responsibility also falls on the mother. It is a team effort; a husband and wife stand strongest when they are joined together. The Bible says in Matthew 18:19-20, "Again I say unto you, That if two of you shall agree on earth as touching any thing that they shall ask, it shall be done for them of my Father which is in heaven. For where two or three are gathered together in my name, there am I in the midst of them." When God's people stand unified for a cause that God desires and call upon the Lord, God is with them. God will enable you to fulfill His will to raise your children for Him. How can we do this? By being a good, consistent role model, asking for God's help, and teaching them regularly.

Guidelines for Choosing
Good Christian Music

Everyone has their personal preferences and opinions on what is good Christian music, and there are disagreements in Christian circles about this. We need to seek the answer to this question by searching the scriptures, coupled with praying to God.

The Bible says in Psalms 30:4, "Sing unto the Lord, O ye saints of his, and give thanks at the remembrance of his holiness." The word *sing* in this verse means to make music with instruments, accompanied by the voice, for the purpose of celebration in song in order to give praise. In this verse, we sing unto the Lord for the purpose of giving thanks unto God for His holiness—praising Him for who He is! Psalms 13:6 says, "I will sing unto the Lord, because he hath dealt bountifully with me." We should sing unto the Lord for what He has done in our lives personally. The Bible says in Psalms 21:13, "Be thou exalted, Lord, in thine own strength: so will we sing and praise thy power." We should sing and praise God for His strength, might, and power.

The Bible says in Psalms 33:2, "Praise the Lord with harp: sing unto him with the psaltery and an instrument of ten strings." We should praise God with instruments.

While looking up various sources within the Bible about music, the statements "sing unto the Lord," "praise unto the Lord," and "rejoice in the Lord" are found. I noticed that they sang, praised, and rejoiced in God because of who He is, because of what He has done to them and for them, and because of His wonderful character. Based on those Scriptures in their proper context, I conclude in the statement below a definition and a rule for distinguishing good Christian music from the bad.

Good Christian music is music that focuses on God and praises God. It is doctrinally correct. It is music that encourages us to be mindful of who God is and what He has done. It will lift up His wonderful character and encourage us to continue to seek and trust Him with our lives. It is music that teaches and expresses biblical truth.

Some prefer a certain genre over another, and some may listen to a variety of genres. But rather than argue about which style or genre is right, we should allow God's guidelines to determine what is best for us. I have found that many types of genres and certain artist meet God's criteria. (We need to take care not to choose music based on the popularity and ability of an artist. Instead, use God's Word to lead us to the right music.)

*Tip: I recommend that you do not immediately introduce just any music into your family, but preview it privately to discern whether or not it is appropriate for your family. I practice this myself, and many times when I have taken the time to listen carefully to the music I have found that the music and singing sounds good but is doctrinally incorrect. Because of this, I would not allow it into my home. (Not everything that looks good is actually good, but also not necessarily everything that appears to be bad is bad.)

We need to teach our children God's perspective on godly music and not solely our own so that, when they are no longer under our authority, they can distinguish between the good and the bad.

Communication between Parents and Their Children

The Bible speaks often about how we should communicate with one another. Proper communication is an important skill to learn and to develop. We need to understand that there are two primary ways we communicate with others: verbal and non-verbal.

We can say one thing, yet convey a completely different message to others with our body language. Being able to communicate with others effectively is important, and when we are able to express our thoughts to others it will help us in all areas of life. Our conversation, as believers, should be the type of communication that edifies others. The word *edify* means "to build." Our communication should be building others up, not tearing them down. This truth is expressed in Ephesians 4:29: "Let no corrupt communication proceed out of your mouth, but that which is good to the use of edifying, that it may minister grace unto the hearers." Our communication with our children should be building them up, teaching them the Word of God in a practical way, helping them to strengthen weak areas in their character, and encouraging them to live for the Lord.

We need to be careful how we speak to our children. There is nothing wrong with a firm tone of voice or raising your voice in such a manner to get your point across. But I believe the line is crossed when it is done in anger and aggression or when a parent belittles and antagonizes them. It is no longer a process of building them up, but we begin to tear them down, causing our children to become so upset that they miss the purpose of the correction. The purpose of correction, discipline, and instruction is to educate and to equip our children with the necessary tools to be successful according to God's standards.

How then should we speak to our children? We need to respect them. We need to truly listen to them and, by doing so, let them know that their thoughts are important to us and that they can come to us about anything.

We should treat them the way we desire for others to treat us. The Bible says in Matthew 7:12, "Therefore all things whatsoever ye would that men should do to you, do ye even so to them: for this is the law and the prophets." We should not treat our children as if they are equal in authority with us, but simply treat them in a manner in which we ourselves would like others to treat us. We want others to respect and listen to us, and we should respect and listen to them.

I am not my child's friend first; I am their parent. This means that my authority should be respected, and then I can be a friend to whom they can express their heart. Some parents attempt to be their child's friend first, but that child does not listen to their parent's instructions, and they completely disregard their parent's authority. By obeying God and applying His word, you can have a balanced relationship with your children where there is harmony, respect, obedience, and a loving atmosphere on a consistent basis.

The saying "Sticks and stones may break my bones, but words will never hurt me" is simply not true. Depending on the injury, physical pain over time can fade, but words tend to leave life-long scars if not dealt with appropriately. Words are powerful,

and with our words we can encourage others or destroy the ones we say we love!

We need to be careful of our tone and language towards our children when we are disciplining them. We do not need to scream and yell at them or be verbally disrespectful to them as we discipline them. (There is nothing wrong with using a firm tone, but there is a clear difference between a firm tone and yelling, screaming, and being verbally disrespectful to them.) Our children should sense our love for them even when we correct them. The Bible says in Proverbs 13:24, "He that spareth his rod hateth his son: but he that loveth him chasteneth him betimes." We correct our children because we love them, and we should correct them in a loving manner according to God's instruction. Talking to our children in a good manner should not just apply when we discipline them, but in our everyday communication with them.

When we interact with others and we know that they care for us, we are better able to receive what they are saying to us. (Even if what is said or done offends the person we are correcting, they can still receive it better knowing of our care for them.)

Mannerisms:

We need to be conscious of our mannerisms when we communicate with others because our body language sometimes says more than the words we say. The attitude in which we say something can hinder the message we are attempting to get across.

Having a Godly View of Our Children

We should learn to view our children from God's perspective and not solely our own, because sometimes without realizing it we may start to lift up our children higher than we should. We can also miss some important things that are happening in their lives that need to be addressed. You could blind yourself to the imperfections in them that need to be seen in order to help them and guide them appropriately. There is nothing wrong with being proud and joyful about our children's conduct—it feels good to see your children consistently doing what is right! But we need to be careful not to allow our pride and love to distort our perception of our children. Sometimes parents with a distorted view of their child will raise them in a manner that will cultivate ungodly behavior or character. There is also the possibility that, if we are not paying close enough attention to our children, we can miss the negative areas in their heart that can cause them to walk down a dark path in life. Let us attempt to view our children from God's perspective so that we may point them in the correct direction in life.

Parents need to be on guard against developing an attitude that believes their children can do no wrong. When confronted by God or men, we should have a heart to check into it before making a judgment call in favor of our children.

There is a clear difference between being an encourager to our children and thinking that they can do no wrong. Believing that they can do no wrong can cause them to develop pride or become self-centered or vain. There is a fine line between building their self-esteem and causing them to view themselves higher than they should.

In order for us not to be deceived, parents need to take the time to know their children. Know the good and bad parts of their character so you can help them in the areas where they are weak and encourage them in the areas they are strong. For example, I remember working with a four-year-old boy whom I will call "J." I worked with "J" since he was a toddler, and I continued to work with him when he moved up to the preschool room. The negative behavior he exhibited early in his life continued and become worse. Throughout that time, the teachers (including myself) had documented that child's behavior for the parents to review, and we verbally informed the parents of their child's consistent poor behavior. **(When I have the opportunity to talk with parents, I like to use the method of positive, negative, positive. If possible, start the conversation out with something positive, then discuss the negative, and then end the conversation with positive comments concerning the child. Using this method, often things are well received by parents concerning their child's negative behavior.)**

Daily, "J" would verbally disrespect teachers and children around him by speaking harshly to them, yelling at them, spitting, and hitting the staff and children. He would not follow directions, attempted on several occasions to run out of the room, and, because of his

aggressive actions, we had to place him in a nurturing hold period-
ically. We attempted to redirect him and positively reinforce good
behavior through various reward systems. We also tried to teach him
about good character and respecting others. He was evaluated by a
counselor, and he was found to be normal. After these processes,
we had a series of meetings with the parents, to discuss the severity
of the behavior and to work together to develop a plan to help. We
assigned an extra staff to shadow. **(I included all this information
to show that we attempted to exhaust various methods to correct that child's poor behavior, for the betterment of the child
and his parents. That is the standard for all young people in our
care.)**

Despite what was shared about "J's" behavior and the steps that
were taken to help him, the parent still expressed disbelief. They
accused teachers of singling him out, implying that teachers were
not being truthful and were the cause of "J's" misconduct.

The parent had the opportunity to view video footage of the inci-
dents. Even when presented with evidence, "J's" parents did not
want to believe the facts and blamed the staff and management. The
child's behavior went on for months. Regardless of what plan or
treatment was implemented, the outcome was the same, and there is
only so much you can do as a caregiver in that type of environment.

*One day, J was acting out during nap time, disrupting the other
children and making it difficult for them to sleep. We tried to provide quiet activities for him and also allowed him to choose the
quiet activity, but the results were the same, and he was redirected.
We tried a reward system; we praised him more for his positive
behavior. Over a period of time, when his behavior did not change,
we had to contact his parents again. His mother came in to check on
him. I explained the situation, and she refused to believe me. She
asked "J" and he confessed. She began to blame other children, and
implied that he is learning this behavior from them. She accused
us of singling out her child until he started acting out in front of

her, and she was unable to correct his behavior. The source of the problem was the lack of proper discipline, good teaching, and lack of attention at home.

The Bible says in Proverbs 13:24, "He that spareth his rod hateth his son: but he that loveth him chasteneth him betimes." *Betimes* means "early." We need to begin training our children early.

We need to take the time to truly know our children and correct negative behavior early. The Bible says in Proverbs 22:6, "Train up a child in the way he should go: and when he is old, he will not depart from it." We need to be teaching and training our children because *"children learn by what we say, what we do, and what we do not correct!"* A child left to his own devices can potentially be disastrous. The Bible says in Proverbs 22:15, "Foolishness is bound in the heart of a child; but the rod of correction shall drive it far from him." The Bible also says in Proverbs 29:15, "The rod and reproof give wisdom: but a child left to himself bringeth his mother to shame."

Children need guidance from their parents, and it is important to take the time to know your beloved children so you can effectively love and lead them in the right direction in life.

Balanced standards, principles, and rules are essential in governing our homes and other areas of society. We need to ask ourselves if the standards, principles, and rules that we have are Bible based. Can the things that you teach be found in the Scriptures? We need to implement standards, principles, and rules in the right balance because, if we are too extreme or too slack, we can cause our children to willfully walk away from the faith of the Lord Jesus Christ. Can the things that you teach be clearly substantiated by the Bible?

Encouraging Our Children To Do What Is Right Publicly and Privately

A concern for many parents is how their children behave when they are unattended and when they are around their peers. God has given me four principles to share that, if applied, can encourage our children to make good decisions.

1.) Applying good, godly discipline. Physical discipline should be applied consistently because it will reinforce your teachings and encourage them to obey. We need to repeatedly take time to teach them what is right.

2.) Teaching the truth that God is omnipresent (present everywhere at the same time). There is nothing anyone can hide from God, and it is important to help them realize that God will hold us accountable for what we do. The Bible says in Ecclesiastes 12:13-14, "Let us hear the conclusion of the whole matter: Fear God, and keep his commandments: for this is the whole duty of man. For God shall bring every work into judgment, with every secret thing, whether it be good, or whether it be evil." 2 Corinthians 5:10 says, "For we must all appear before the judgment seat of Christ; that every one may receive the things done in his body, according to that he hath done, whether it be good or bad." We should teach our children to do what is right whether they are alone or with others because God is always watching. We all should be conscious of this truth and, by doing so, we will make better choices.

"Do what is right whether someone is there or not because God is always watching."

3.) Teaching our children that, when they obey their parents, it pleases us and (most importantly) God. The Bible says in Ephesians 6:1, "Children, obey your parents in the Lord: for this is right." The Bible says in Colossians 3:20, "Children, obey your parents in all things: for this is well pleasing unto the Lord."

4.) Rewarding our children for doing what is right, but not confusing a reward system with a system of bribery. When my children do what is right on their own, I will reward them. That reward encourages them to continue doing what is right, just as God will reward His people for their obedience to His will. (Understand that there is a thin line between a bribery system and a reward system. Bribery says that, in order for a person to do what is right, they have to be offered something first, but a reward is given because a person choose to do right in the beginning.)

I used to have a boss that would say, "Trust, but verify." I would think, if they trusted me, why would they need to verify what I am doing? I considered it to be a hypocritical statement she made! But I think it is an appropriate statement if you believe it to mean, "I trust you, but I need to observe you and check up on you from time to time in order to verify that you are doing what is right and to ensure you continue to walk down the right path." We need to have that type of attitude concerning our children. My beloved children have proven themselves to be trustworthy, but because they have a sin nature I check on them from time to time in order to keep them walking on the right path. Remember, no one is perfect! The Bible says in Proverbs 22:15, "Foolishness is bound in the heart of a child; but the rod of correction shall drive it far from him." Knowing the truth about my children concerning their heart's condition, I take the time to check on them to encourage them to walk and stay on the right path. The Bible says in Proverbs 29:15, "The rod and reproof give wisdom: but a child left to himself bringeth his mother to shame." It is good to know that people care enough about you to hold you accountable and attempt to encourage you. I find that, when people do that, it helps us to stay aware of our actions and words.

Weeding Out Jealousy
between Siblings

Jealousy between siblings can be prevented. If you notice it developing in your children, you can correct them, so they do not develop a jealous heart toward their siblings or others.

Jealousy between siblings can occur when one is treated better than the other. A good biblical example for this can be found in Genesis 37:2-4. That passage tells us about Israel (the father) showing favoritism to Joseph, who was one out of many children that Israel had. The Bible says in Genesis 37:2-4,

> These are the generations of Jacob. Joseph, being seventeen years old, was feeding the flock with his brethren; and the lad was with the sons of Bilhah, and with the sons of Zilpah, his father's wives: and Joseph brought unto his father their evil report. Now Israel loved Joseph more than all his children, because he was the son of his old age: and he made him a coat of many colours. And when his brethren saw that their father loved him more than all his brethren, they hated him, and could not speak peaceably unto him.

You and I need to be careful how we treat our children. Showing favoritism can ruin the relationship between siblings.

Showing favoritism is different from treating them uniquely because of their age difference and developmental requirements. For example, I have two sons who are about seven years apart. I remember my oldest son being concerned about the amount of attention given to his younger brother. I explained to him that, when he was that same age, I treated him the same way. Because he is older, I am preparing him for the next stage of his life! I reminded him that my love for him is the same. I still showed affection through hugs, kisses, time spent with them, discipline, and instruction.

*Jealousy can occur between siblings when one sibling becomes envious of the other's talents (a special natural ability) or skills (ability coming from one's knowledge and practice), when one receives praise because of his character traits, or when one person is being treated better than another. We see an example in Genesis 4:1-13:

> And Adam knew Eve his wife; and she conceived, and bare Cain, and said, I have gotten a man from the Lord. And she again bare his brother Abel. And Abel was a keeper of sheep, but Cain was a tiller of the ground. And in process of time it came to pass, that Cain brought of the fruit of the ground an offering unto the Lord. And Abel, he also brought of the firstlings of his flock and of the fat thereof. And the Lord had respect unto Abel and to his offering: But unto Cain and to his offering he had not respect. And Cain was very wroth, and his countenance fell. And the Lord said unto Cain, Why art thou wroth? And why is thy countenance fallen? If thou doest well, shalt thou not be accepted? And if thou doest not well, sin lieth at the door. And unto thee shall be his desire, and thou shalt rule over him. And Cain talked with Abel his brother: and it came to pass, when they were in the field, that Cain rose up against Abel his brother, and slew him. And the Lord said unto Cain, Where is Abel thy brother? And he said, I know not: Am I my brother's keeper? And he said, What

hast thou done? The voice of thy brother's blood crieth unto me from the ground. And now art thou cursed from the earth, which hath opened her mouth to receive thy brother's blood from thy hand; When thou tillest the ground, it shall not henceforth yield unto thee her strength; a fugitive and a vagabond shalt thou be in the earth. And Cain said unto the Lord , My punishment is greater than I can bear.

We see that Abel's offering was received, but Cain's offering was not. Cain became furious and murdered his brother. We need to be careful not to sin because we might feel a certain way! The Bible says in Ephesians 4:26, "Be ye angry, and sin not: let not the sun go down upon your wrath:" Through this scripture, God allowed me to teach my sons that it is okay for them to feel the way they feel, but it is not okay to do what is wrong because we are upset! God enabled me to guide them through that emotional state by doing the following:

1.) Encouraging them to realize and acknowledge feelings in their heart.

2.) Teaching them by instruction and by deliberate actions that we will not always be able to get what we want, nor will we always be able to have what someone else has!

3.) Teaching them and encouraging them to be content instead of focusing on what they do not have, and to look at what God has blessed them with. I created a devotional on the topic using Philippians 4:11-13, instilling in them that we have to learn how to be content no matter where we find ourselves in life. I taught my children that it is not going to be easy all the time, but you can do all things through (and with) Christ if you allow Him to work in your life, especially in the areas in which you struggle.

4.) Praying to God about the situation. God wants His people to cast their cares and burdens upon Him because He cares for us. He is concerned for us and desires to be there for His people, but we need to allow Him to work in our hearts and lives (1 Peter 5:7; Matthew 11:28-30).

5.) Talking with someone about what is going on in their heart. Because God has placed people in our lives to be of help to us, we should choose people prayerfully and carefully. We should choose someone who is more spiritually mature, someone that has gone through and come out of a similar situation. They were able to overcome because they applied the Word of God.

By conducting devotional time on this topic and many others, God has been able to work in my children's hearts, changing their thinking regarding this matter.

Parents, if you are the cause of your children's jealousy toward one another, you need to get that right with God and your children. From this point on, begin to love them equally in a manner that pleases God. Understand that there will be differences in the way we treat our children, but we should never favor one over another.

Cultivating a Sincere
Heart of Apology

We cannot force a child in his heart to mean the things he says, but we can provide the right environment for his heart to be developed correctly.

As a caregiver for over fourteen years, I have witnessed many occasions in which parents have forced their children to apologize to others that they have wronged. In the majority of cases, those children have not been sincere at all, and it is evident that the apology had no meaning to them. I have seen some children that have had no remorse for what they have done! They just said what their parents expected them to say. I believe this is because those parents have not taught their children the significance of why we apologize and how it affects them and the other party involved. Most parents teach the mechanical aspect of it by instructing them to just simply say, "I am sorry."

I have found the opposite to be true because of the lessons taught from the Word of God. In the beginning of this book, I stressed the importance of teaching the Word of God and teaching our children the Word in such a way that they can understand it, relate to it, and apply it to their own lives. In order to develop a sincere heart of apology in a child, we must first teach lessons on that topic. The

Bible says in Matthew 5:23-26, "Therefore if thou bring thy gift to the altar, and there rememberest that thy brother hath ought against thee; Leave there thy gift before the altar, and go thy way; first be reconciled to thy brother, and then come and offer thy gift. Agree with thine adversary quickly, whiles thou art in the way with him; lest at any time the adversary deliver thee to the judge, and the judge deliver thee to the officer, and thou be cast into prison. Verily I say unto thee, Thou shalt by no means come out thence, till thou hast paid the uttermost farthing."

In this text of scripture, we see the importance of getting things right with the one that you have wronged in order to take care of the issue while it is small, before it becomes a larger one. Teaching this principle in our devotional time has helped to develop a sincere heart in my children. When opportunity arises, show them the importance of applying this truth whether they have wronged someone or someone has wronged them. The Bible also says in Luke 17:3-4, "Take heed to yourselves: If thy brother trespass against thee, rebuke him; and if he repent, forgive him. And if he trespass against thee seven times in a day, and seven times in a day turn again to thee, saying, I repent; thou shalt forgive him." It is important to teach our children about the serious matter of forgiveness and for us to practice and demonstrate to our children a sincere heart of apology. There have been times when I was wrong, and I chose to apologize to my children. When I did, I found that my relationship with my children became stronger because there was a deeper respect given to me. Through this scripture, we can learn the following: If someone has wronged you, it is important to express yourself respectfully to that individual, letting them know what issue they caused. If that individual apologizes for that wrong, be willing to forgive them. Regardless of how many times an individual has wronged you, be willing to forgive them. Be wise and be willing to forgive but not forget. When you truly forgive someone for something, there should not be any ill will concerning that person.

Luke 11:4 says, "And forgive us our sins; for we also forgive every one that is indebted to us. And lead us not into temptation; but deliver us from evil." Colossians 3:13 says, "Forbearing one another, and forgiving one another, if any man have a quarrel against any: even as Christ forgave you, so also do ye."

Ephesians 4:32 says, "And be ye kind one to another, tenderhearted, forgiving one another, even as God for Christ's sake hath forgiven you." I used the Scriptures above to teach my son that we should choose to forgive others because Christ has forgiven us for the wrong we have done! Because of what Jesus Christ has done and who He is, we should be willing and able to forgive others. This should be our motivation.

I also taught them about the dangers of bitterness developing in the heart. Hebrews 12:15 says, "Looking diligently lest any man fail of the grace of God; lest any root of bitterness springing up trouble you, and thereby many be defiled." Bitterness comes when people do not talk to one another to work out issues they have with each other. Bitterness develops when a person does not forgive another for the hurt he has caused. Bitterness is the gateway to hate! Below are some ways I taught my children how to express themselves in order to prevent and deal appropriately with bitterness:

1.) "Mess up, 'fess up." When you do something wrong, confess it and get it right with that individual.

2.) If there is an issue between you and another person, go and talk to them. Do not go to anyone else but the one with whom you have the issue. I also tell my children not to expect them to agree with you that they have done wrong. The focus is to express what the problem is respectfully and factually. Try to leave out emotional statements such as "I feel." People will argue opinions and feelings, but when you focus on the facts of a situation, people may not be as quick to argue.

3.) When you communicate with others, attempt to be clear and straight to the point.

Expressing Love to Our Children

The Bible says in Ephesians 6:4, "And, ye fathers, provoke not your children to wrath: but bring them up in the nurture and admonition of the Lord."

God impressed upon my heart to focus on the matter of parental expression—loving and nurturing our children, showing affection to our children in public and in private. (Nurturing means "to encourage, train and educate our children, pointing them in the right direction in this life.") Often in our society, men show children (especially boys) how to be tough. Conversely, the women are the ones that show affection to their children. I know that there are exceptions to this, where the opposite is true.

As parents, both need to learn to express love toward children. It will help in your children's development and it is an example that they will use when they raise their children and interact with their spouses. We need to understand that children need both their father and mother. Both parents have important things to teach and contribute to their lives.

Parents show love to their children by verbally expressing it to them and by demonstrating it to their children consistently. The Bible is God's love letter to us. Throughout the Bible, God expresses His love to us, and He ultimately demonstrated His love on Calvary. He also demonstrates His love for His children by listening to our prayers, answering our prayers, comforting us, instructing and guiding us.

We need to tell our children that we love them. We need to discipline them, provide and enforce rules, and be consistent in correcting them when needed. We must keep our word and encourage them when they have done what is right.

We need to demonstrate our love by spending time with them. We should listen to them and take an interest in what they are interested in, especially when that interest is a positive one. We need to reassure them with our words and actions, just like God demonstrates His love to us.

I have been to many churches, and I notice often that mainly mothers openly express their love and appreciation for their children. I want to encourage men to also openly express (in a balanced manner) their heart to their children. Through a parent's example, children will learn how to express themselves in similar ways to their families.

Building Self-Confidence

The best way to build up our children's self-esteem is by teaching them about how God thinks about them. God's Word is powerful and is able to touch and change the heart. We need to tell our children what we think of them as well, because God uses us as an instrument to build up others, especially our children.

I recall one day that my oldest son came home from school, and I could tell that something was bothering him. He had a sad countenance and his behavior was unusual; he was not himself.

I asked him what was wrong, and at first he was hesitant. I reminded him that I am always here for him and that I want to help him. (In a similar manner, we need to remember that God is always there for His people.) I stated that the only thing stopping him from talking to me was himself, just like the only thing that stops a Christian from gaining access to God is our unconfessed sin and our unwillingness to ask for forgiveness. The Bible says in Psalms 66:18, "If I regard iniquity in my heart, the Lord will not hear me." It also says in 1 John 1:9, "If we confess our sins, he is faithful and just to forgive us our sins, and to cleanse us from all unrighteousness."

After saying those things, he shared with me that he was being teased and that children were making him feel bad because of how he talked (he had difficulty expressing himself to his peers).

I attempted to encourage him, but God impressed upon my heart to encourage him through His Word. As I was praying for my son, God led me to a scripture passage for a Bible lesson to teach my son, which was Psalms 139:14, "I will praise thee; for I am fearfully and wonderfully made: marvellous are thy works; and that my soul knoweth right well." I taught my son through that text that God had made him, and that the way He made him is good.

God showed me the importance of studying my children, and I recognized some things about him that made it difficult for him when he attempted to interact with others. I began to teach and build him up in the areas of character and behavior that were weak, and I taught him from the Scriptures and gave him rules and principles to apply to make his interaction with others more successful. I also challenged and encouraged him through this statement: *"Don't let people define you; what should define you is the Word of God. The opinion of the Lord is the only opinion that truly matters."*

After a period of time I noticed that his self-esteem grew and his interaction with his peers and others became more successful.

Authority in the Home

God has created the family structure and, in His great wisdom, has placed the man as the head of the family, then the wife, and lastly the children. Often that pattern is ignored, and when we do the opposite of God's plan and God's design we will experience unnecessary hardship. If you have more than one child, I want to encourage you to employ a system of authority among them. This can be accomplished by giving the older authority over the younger. It is important for the eldest to guide properly using good, godly methods that you have modeled and taught them from the Word of God. At times, the younger siblings may rebel against their eldest sibling's authority, so you will have to use biblical discipline to encourage them to obey. If your eldest child is not using their authority properly, correct them and show them the proper way to guide their siblings in that situation. I also instructed my youngest child that if the older brother told him to do something that is wrong, he had my permission to disobey. Doing this can help siblings develop a good relationship with one another.

Teaching Siblings How to Get Along

Psalms 133:1-3 says, "Behold, how good and how pleasant it is for brethren to dwell together in unity! It is like the precious ointment upon the head, that ran down upon the beard, even Aaron's beard: that went down to the skirts of his garments; As the dew of Hermon, and as the dew that descended upon the mountains of Zion: for there the Lord commanded the blessing, even life for evermore."

Teaching brothers and sisters how to work well with each other is important and beneficial to parents, but especially to siblings. Teaching them how to properly interact with one another will build and strengthen their relationship. We need to be good friends with people that God has placed in our lives and encourage our children to be good friends to others, especially with their siblings. Having worked with children of all ages for many years, I have worked with many parents that believe that it is acceptable for their children to fight regularly with one another. That should not be the normal type of relationship that is allowed within your home. Realistically, children will have some level of conflict with one another, but it should not be behavior that is consistently observed.

The Bible says in Proverbs 27:17, "Iron sharpeneth iron; so a man sharpeneth the countenance of his friend." Our children should have a relationship with one another that strengthens and encourages each other. It should be a relationship that gets better over time. Children who know Jesus Christ as their personal Savior can encourage one another to grow in faith, moving forward for the Lord.

The Bible says in Proverbs 18:24, "A man that hath friends must shew himself friendly: and there is a friend that sticketh closer than a brother." In this scripture, we can easily see Jesus Christ as the wonderful friend that sticketh closer than a brother. We can also see that God tells us that, in order to have (and keep) a friend, we need to treat them right. That is also what we need to instill in our children. In order to have a good relationship with their siblings, they must treat them right.

The Bible says in Proverbs 17:17, "A friend loveth at all times, and a brother is born for adversity." It is important to teach our children to express affection to their siblings and to be there for each other in the difficult moments in life, knowing they can depend on one another.

We need to teach our children not to cover up the wrong that a sibling may do, but rather to help them to do what is right, exposing the moral weaknesses in their siblings' heart in order for it to be corrected. I taught this principle to my children because, although it is natural to want to protect your siblings, some children think it is acceptable to lie for their brother or sister. But I explained to my children that, when you do that, you will eventually hurt the very one you are trying to protect. What if that very behavior you lied about to protect your sibling turns out to be the very thing that they do that damages their life or someone else's?

Being a parent can be challenging and rewarding. We should think about what we want to impart to our children. We should not be the type of parent that just responds to what is happening with our children. Rather think ahead about what type of person you would like to help them to become and what you can do to instill and develop this nature. The Bible has the answer. God will show you how to raise your children. God will help you from start to finish if you rely on Him alone. The Bible says in Philippians 1:6, "Being confident of this very thing, that he which hath begun a good work in you will perform [or "finish"] it until the day of Jesus Christ." God wants you to succeed, but that success can only come by obeying God and allowing Him to guide you as you raise your children.